Lost in a Dream

by

Kelly Anne

DORRANCE
PUBLISHING CO
EST. 1920
PITTSBURGH, PENNSYLVANIA 15238

Dorrance Publishing Co
585 Alpha Drive
Suite 103
Pittsburgh, PA 15238
Visit our website at *www.dorrancebookstore.com*

ISBN: 978-1-4809-3032-2
eISBN: 978-1-4809-3010-0

1981

"**C**ome on, Kelly! Come with us!"

I looked down the dark hallway. I was upstairs in my grandmother's house. Everyone downstairs was sleeping, my mom, sister, grandma, grandpa, aunt, and uncle. There I was, looking into a hole under the bathroom sink, where I could see another world. It was like another dimension. But in the bathroom? Silly dreams...but this was...real? It reminded me of the churchyard next door to my apartment house. There they were, the children of the world playing soccer. Black, White, Asian, Spanish, Arab—every nation, even the blue-eyed German girl with pigtails. All were smiling and laughing playing together.

"I can't go!" I called out to them, knowing I wouldn't know how to get back. It sounded like I was calling out to the universe. My voice didn't sound the same. It was like I was yelling through a hole.

I looked down the dark hall again. Why was I afraid to leave this world? I wanted to go. I almost made the leap. Something stopped me. I looked back again. My family would miss me, and I would probably get in trouble anyway because I always did. But I liked this world. At a young age, I knew I didn't want to leave it. But I always knew I wanted to go "home." Wherever that is.

"I'll see you guys soon!" I called out to them.

"Okay, we'll be here, Kelly!" The dark boy smiled at me, waved goodbye, and carried on kicking the ball to make the goal.

I woke up on the couch in my grandmother's living room, where I fell asleep. The grandfather clock was going off. It was 6 A.M. The curtains were

1

blowing from the breeze. I still remember the smell. The sweet air that smelled like grass and flowers, the way the curtains smelled because they have been washed. It was my grandma's house. I can still smell her perfume. I don't know what brand she wore and have not found the scent up to today. But sometimes I can smell it when there's no one around.

I looked around. It was so much cleaner than where I lived. I could see the marks on my arm from the sheets, and I felt them on my face. You know when you wake from a deep sleep. My body felt so heavy. Like my soul lifted out of my body and went "elsewhere." I took a deep breath and sat up. Everyone was still sleeping. The sun was coming up. The dream felt so real. I was five. That was my first "real" dream. The last bell sounded.

Right around that time, I can remember a black eight ball coming right at me. I was in my bed. My sister was asleep right next to me in our one-little-bedroom apartment. She didn't see or hear me. I tried to push it away but was helpless, as it didn't seem real—more like an illusion because I wasn't asleep and nothing was coming at me in the "real world." After that there were the other dreams, where things actually happened. Sometimes they would come in my dreams, sometimes I wasn't asleep.

I remember during a drive to my great-grandmother's house to Brooklyn, I fell asleep in my grandparents' car. While looking up at the sky, I started to close my eyes. I saw a ballroom dance. It was like one of my real dreams, like I was there. I was a princess ready to come down the stairs but wanted to watch the people dance. I felt beautiful and saw I was in a glamourous ballroom. I was leaning over the marble balcony, smiling. The beautiful gowns and corsets dancing around the floor. I knew I was in a castle. The women were dressed like ladies. I felt like I was dreaming of a past life. They were dancing and smiling. I awoke to walking through wrought-iron gates with a vegetable garden in the little concrete backyard. Brooklyn. Brown stones so beautifully put together. There were people around. The boys playing in the streets. But us, we had to go right in. You can smell the Sunday Sauce as soon as you walked in. My great-grandma would kiss you right in the ear to make it ring! The times I remember seeing her, she did that. Who is ever really prepared for a kiss like that? A ring-right-in-the-ear kiss" You get ready to block it, but they get you every time.

I started to see things different from others. Was I the one who was different? I tried to find my place in this world. But when I looked at others I

saw, I was always missing something. A feeling inside me. Like I didn't belong anywhere. Even at my young age.

I like to call them the Italian days of summer in Elmont. My grandfather
playing Italian music in the living room and sauce on the stove in my
grandma and grandpas house. It smelled Italian. The love was so simple. My
Uncle had Down syndrome. We had the best laughs. Me and my sister would
literally climb right over him when he tried to hide under the sewing machine
when playing hide-and-seek pretending not to see him. Or the slide on the
plastic pool came down, spilling all the water out because he sat right on it.
Innocence. But he was…my family. It smelled like love all throughout the
house. Especially up the stairs, down the hall, where the bathroom was. It
was hard to explain. The food, the music, fruit in the trees, charcoal bbq's,
sausage on a fork. The good old days of summer in Elmont. The airplanes
flew right over Hill Avenue. I remember looking up, watching them pass
over the house and the huge tree in the driveway. The planes were so loud
we couldn't hear ourselves!

Elmont was a split neighborhood back then. Today it seems every na-
tionality lives there and all over. But when I was little, the black people lived
on the north side of the main road, Black Elmont , and white people lived
on the south side but we all went to school together. My grandma lived on
the South Side. It was predominately Italian and Irish. Middle class. I was in
the middle. I saw both sides. The church next door was in the middle, too.
Depending on where you lived. There was also the volunteer fire department.
I was so proud of them, the men they were. I can remember Richie jumping
right over the gate to run to the firetruck when the alarm went off. On Sun-
days after mass, the boys from the neighborhood played football in the
churchyard. I used to hang on the gate and watch them. What if the ball flew
over my gate? Right? Maybe the soccer dream had something to do with
watching "the guys" playing "American football." But I dreamt of the soccer
field way before I saw these guys plus they weren't from all over the world.
I remember one always came over to say hello. They called to him, "Hey,
your girlfriend is looking for you." He would come over. So sweet. Why
would I ask for a guy to come to me? As a psychologist would say, you don't
have a male figure in your life. But did I need one?

The airplanes frequently flew right over the soccer field/churchyard.
They weren't so loud by my apartment but flew right over. I remember look-

ing at them, running with them, and falling in the grass, smelling that it was just cut. I would watch the wheels come down, watching the plane descending, getting ready to land at JFK. The wheels looked like a guy hanging from them. I asked my mom if that was a guy hanging from the plane. Of course, my mother said there was no way. They wouldn't make it. I'm sure I asked her why and a hundred more questions. I still stared at the planes, knowing or maybe wishing someone would come here on one day, for me. It was a strong feeling.

Growing up wasn't easy for me. My mom was a single mother and I had a sister, who was a year older than me. We were poor, and the kids from the neighborhood reminded me every day. Being by my grandparents' house were happy times for me and my sister.

I remember after a horrible day at school, I was walking past the churchyard. The sun was about to set. I looked up at the sky to ask God to make my life better. I didn't want to be poor. I didn't want the other kids to tease me and my sister. Why were people, kids so mean and full of hate? I did have some friends who were just like me. We didn't have much, but we always had fun with what we had. It's like some people act like they are better than you because they have more money or a "together family."

I wanted the world to be a beautiful place like the kids playing soccer in my dream. They were laughing and smiling. I guess I still had my childlike innocence. They say in life you should never lose that. The part where there is peace and love in your heart, innocence. They weren't mocking each other because of who or what they were or because they were different from one another.

We were learning about war in school. There was a lot of fighting around the world and we were at war with Russia. It was the start of the Cold War. Remembering my day, two boys pretended to gun me down with machine guns since I was part Russian. Jerks! I asked God, "Please make me beautiful" (I thought that would make them stop teasing me). Sometimes it seems people don't realize it's not what you look like but who you are.

I said to myself, "I want the world to be happy—no more fighting, no more hate, God." That was when I saw a star fall from the sky. My wish was going to come true but when, how? A shooting star just like something in a fairytale. Had God heard me? I looked around. No one else saw it. It was just for me to see. I had a great feeling in me that everything was going to be okay. It had to be a signal. A sign of hope. A sign from God. Then I went home.

My mom would occasionally visit an elderly lady in the senior center to keep her company. Of course, my sister and I had to go. We were seven and eight then. It was so boring. One summer day, I remember we were there watching TV. We were only allowed to sit on the couch. There was nothing else to do. It had that old lady smell and look. A dusty place with outdated furniture and a mothball musty smell. I went to the window. I placed my hands on the windowsill and placed my chin on my hands while looking out. There was a house on the other side of the gate behind the senior center. The screen was hard to look out, maybe because it was so dirty or it was so hot it seemed that way. It was a big, well-kept house. I saw an in-ground pool with a slide. "Wow, I wish I could go in there." I put my nose really close to the screen to smell the fresh air coming in. Four years later I would be in that pool, but I didn't know about wishes coming true yet. I did know there was something special in the world that others couldn't see, or maybe they just didn't want to see. Making this come true lead to a series of deja vu moments and more dreams coming true.

Christina Silver had to come from Guyana. I was eight years old then. Because I was the most outgoing, we were the same age, and she lived closest to me, Mrs. P asked if I could "show her around." We became good friends. When her family got together, everyone came, and I'm not talking about one aunt and one set of grandparents. I'm talking about eight brothers and a sister, cousins and friends from their hometown in Guyana. Even people from distant parts of the world. I would never forget one of the Aunt's family came from India. This woman was wearing a Suri with sparkles on it. I don't think I left her side that night. Poor woman! The music was from their country, they played it loud. They all got together, celebrated, and danced. There was never fighting, only laughter and celebrations. Christina's grandfather always read from the Bible and gave a speech before the food and celebration started; he was a preacher in Georgetown. He was a little old man with glasses and always dressed in a button down shirt and slacks. They all respected him. Everyone would be like okay, come on already. I guess we were impatient. He preached about God and how this is a test. If we are good here, then we go up to heaven. I believed that, and everyone there knew he was right. The hands were kept folded and eyes closed listening to him, allowing him to finish his words of prayer and thankfulness.

So the Silver's knew the Fox's. There was a party at the Fox's home. We were invited, my mother started "dating" Christina's uncle. We drove down the cul-de-sac. I was never down these streets, yet I passed them all the time. The inside of the house was clean and well taken care of. They were very classy people in the way they acted. Soft spoken and proper. Even their three daughters were prettier than the next. Long flowy dresses, perfect hair and skin. They looked happy through their smiles. Maybe that's what made them prettier. Music was loud, soft jazz music was playing. It was a beautiful night. I knew I was supposed to be here.

They invited us to come the next day to go in the pool. Christina, my sister, Eddie, and I ran to the pool. We were laughing and going down the slide. Who would win the race? We were going down the slide, jumping in the pool as normal kids do. I got out to jump back in again. As I was about to jump, I looked straight ahead, I froze. We were behind the senior center! I saw the window that I was looking out of. I remembered that day years ago when I made that wish to go in this pool. What a coincidence, or maybe my sincere wish did come true! I didn't say anything. That year my brother was born. I was ten.

We were spending so much time with Christina's family that we stopped going to my grandma's house. I was happy that I got to experience new people, but me and my sister missed them. They were our foundation—our family. My aunt married, had two kids, and lived with her husband in grandma's basement. Things were different now.

One night I was home babysitting my baby brother while my mom, stepfather, and sister were out. I was holding him on my bed rocking him to sleep, looking at how beautiful he was. They say children are prophecies. This "thought," or "voice," yet it was so loud it seemed real. It was a man's voice. It said, "Your grandma is going to die." Just like that! Clearly! So loud and clear. "No!" I started crying. Maybe I felt that way because I missed them so much. When my mother came home, I was crying hysterically. "Are you doing drugs?" she yelled at me. What? I was ten!

"Something is going to happen to Grandma!" I yelled at her.

She didn't believe me. I called Grandma the next day. The week after was Thanksgiving. I tried not to cry when I spoke to her.

"Grandma, we haven't seen you guys in so long."

"Come for Thanksgiving!" she said.

Smiling, I said, "Okay, I love you."

I was relieved and passed the phone. It was like I could remember her scent. I'd get to see her and hug her. Except that would be the last time I spoke to her. She fell a few days later, cut her leg, and was admitted in the hospital. She died the night before Thanksgiving. From a cut on the leg on a gutter! They said she had an aneurism and they couldn't save her. I remember the phone ringing, my sister screaming and crying. I went in the backyard. Sat on the abandoned white car. I looked up at the sky, it turned as red as her hair and it started snowing. A record-breaker that year. God, why did you take her from us so soon? She was only fifty-two. I saw my sister running away. I knew where she was going. She ran to our grandma's house. Except she was not there anymore. It would never be the same again. I already knew this was going to happen. I heard the voice, it told me.

A week later, I had another dream where there was a terrible accident. I woke up the next morning. My mother was sitting with her friend. I started to explain what I saw, how someone was thrown out the window and there were firetrucks there. "Oh, stop," my mother said. Her friend said, "No, let her talk." I was always told to be quiet! Did anybody else experience this? My mom's friend ran up to me at church the next morning and told me her nephew was in a terrible accident and he was thrown from the window. She told me it was just like the dream i had. He was in the hospital with internal bleeding. He did live. From that point on, it sometimes felt hard to determine what was a dream and what was reality. I knew I wasn't crazy. I starting seeing actual events before they happened. I had witnesses, experiences.

Sometimes no one believed me, but the "experiences" came true. I was a very smart girl. I could do anything I wanted. I was book and street smart for my young age. I knew I wasn't crazy! I went to the pastor next door to ask him questions. He really didn't answer much. He could only explain the usual that God was always there. I asked him about spirits and messages from God. He didn't have an explanation as to what was happening to me.

I always questioned this. Why if God is there why does bad stuff happen? Looking at peoples behaviors, seeing the way people are and if God is love, then why is there war and destruction on this earth? Seeing the way the world is with all the fighting, earthquakes, and people dying under

Mother Nature's fury, who wouldn't question that? This is a question me and Arturo, Brandy's husband, always talked about. I couldn't win this discussion with him because I didn't have the answer, either.

"He was always there." That was always the answer. That was what I believed and "knew." Was he bored one day and just said, "Oh, let me make these people and see what they do"? I wanted more. I knew there was something more. I wanted to know.

What is the meaning of life, and where do we go after we die?

I told him what I saw, what I felt, I don't think he believed me. No one knew what me and my sister went through, waking up with my mom and stepdad fighting after he got home from the bar, always over money. Go to school with that and try to act normal. I also remember other misfortunate events little girls shouldn't have to go through. What kind of life was I in? I looked around. How can it get better? I found some pills in the bathroom took off the cap and swallowed them down. Except they didn't work. The whole bottle didn't do a thing except make my body jolt. God didn't want me to die, not yet. My "job" wasn't done. I've learned at that point only God should take you when he is ready, when you are ready.

After three high schools in one year, seeing I couldn't really depend on anyone, I tried to fit in, but it didn't seem like I fit in anywhere. I moved to Queens when I was seventeen. Far enough to sound far away. I always remembered my town. I loved going back to visit my mom. Even until this day.

Years later here I am. Seems like times have changed and we are getting older now. Throughout the years, my dreams were always there. Like the time a friend was in a coma and I knew when he was going to wake up. I had a feeling in me that I couldn't describe. One of my aunts called my job, stating she had that feeling, too. My boss said, "Is it me? I'm going on a plane tonight," when he saw me clench my chest. It was hurting, and I was hurting inside. That night my aunt's neighbor was driving with friends. I wasn't that close to him, but we did have some good nights sitting on the steps talking as neighbors. A firetruck hit the car. A young girl died, and my aunt's neighbor was in a coma. We went to visit him in the hospital. A few days later, I had the dream that he woke up. That morning I ran over to his father.

"He's going to wake up! I saw it in my dream last night!" I was so excited.

"I hope so, Kelly," he said.

That day he did! His father came to the house and told us. He hugged me, saying I was right. When I went to visit him right after he woke up, he pulled me toward him. He still couldn't talk and had just woken up. The way he was pulling me made me uncomfortable. Were we in the same dream? Did he see me there? He eventually and slowly was coming back, but you could see he would never be the same again. Why would someone go around pulling fire alarms? This persons actions had ruined lives of good people!

Then there are the times when you dream of someone you haven't seen in fifteen years. With no reason at all, not that you saw a friend who knows them, nothing. That happened a lot, seeing. I didn't tell anyone because they don't believe you anyway! Who could I trust?

6/2009

I have a son. He son is ten now. — His father and I finally came to agreements to separate. I don't understand why people stay together if they aren't meant to. In fact, when I first saw him, I was with my friend Brandy. I knew I couldn't stand him. There is the saying "the end is in the beginning". I guess being in the office with him and us both being in bad relationships, we started to hang out after work. One thing led to another, and that was how my son was born. Apparently, this was the way to go. However, we were one of the biggest insurance agents in the Queens car business. There was also the car lot, repair shop, alarm and cell phone store all in one building. We dealt with people all over the world, and I loved my customers; even our workers were from all over the world. Pakistan, Afghanistan, Israel, Trinidad, the Dominican Republic. We even insured someone from the United Nations. My customers were my friends. Some would come in just to hang out. Muhammad brought us back papyrus scrolls from Egypt with Egyptian inscriptions. I remember him saying his wife couldn't go into the pyramids because she was having a baby. She was smiling while having her hands on her stomach. She was 8 months then. We all got along, all our customers and workers.

My son's father and I had a big beautiful home, a beautiful healthy son, a great business. It was stressful but also exciting. I think the day I lost all respect for him was when he took his middle finger, pointed it up to the sky, and said, "F you," to God! That's the day when I couldn't even be near him. The day I felt I had to protect my son. I realized he didn't even love himself. I remember him talking to one of the girls who worked for us. Walina. I will never forget her. My son's father told her that she was from a third-world country because she came from Afghanistan and they throw sticks and rocks to fight. He had some nerve. I was thinking if there's a lot of people like him, no wonder they hate us, the other countries. I would never forget her face. She stood up to him and said she would go back to fight with her country if she had to.

"That's why all you foreigners don't belong here." He said.

That's when I ended the conversation. I had some power, not enough but only enough to end this conversation. She loved her country like I loved mine. Like he loved Italy even though he was born here. I didn't blame her. It's like when he said I came from Elmont. That it's a poor town because he came from a home with money. He left her alone. How dare you!? I thought looking at him. Plus he was so nice to her father. Hypocrite! When he wasn't there, I remembered her talking about arranged marriages and hoping her father would pick someone kind, good, and cute, she said with a smile. She was a sweet girl. A good girl, kind and smart. I hoped she would have the life she wanted. There are some marriages where the guy beats the girl, hurts her, cheats on her, treats her like a piece of property. Is that how you treat your "property"? There was a girl from India who went through that when Brandy and I worked at the drycleaners when I was 18. She felt like she couldn't get out of it. Until today I think of her and wonder if she's doing ok.

Right before my son and his father split up I had a conversation with one of our workers. He was going through issues too but with his wife. I always enjoyed our talks. We could be honest about things because we both knew the conversation would stay right there. He saw a mark on my arm one day and says you must like it. Like what? I asked. He looked at it and says "well you stay". That's when it "hit" me. The truth was I didn't like it and when he said that to me it gave me strength. Nor did I want my son to think this ok because he's growing up now and I didn't want him to see it thinking this is the way to treat women. I wasn't in an arranged marriage. To stop it, leaving would be the only way. I didn't have to deal with this. I grew a little stronger. One day I fought back and finally left him. I had the biggest weight off my shoulders. Of course he said he would ruin me financially, he did. But that's okay. How much for a free life?

This is about another dream of mine, so real you see it, feel it, like you are there. This is about some guy who was in my dreams but so far away. I feel lost because of the way he has made me feel.

October 10, 2009 2P.M.

*I*t was my weekend off, and my son was by his father's. Get up, make coffee, check emails and social media. I run one of those silly quizzes, who will be my soulmate? Starts with the letter A and born in between April and May. Got it. My friends are "okay" and beautiful. Got myself together to meet Bianca and one of her guy friends. I'll clean later, looking back before I locked my door.

I meet with my friend Bianca. She said to come by her to go to a fair. We went to a local Long Island fair. It was a beautiful day! It was a typical Long Island fair...antiques, food, rides, desserts, families, and laughing children. Then we found the wine tent. We were drinking wine when she did her contacts and said we will go to Bell Blvd. in Queens. Excellent! Yay! I threw my hands up in the air. It was by me—no one to depend on. Take a cab and I'll get home. No problem. Plus I will wake up in my own bed, not my friend's couch, and I would be surrounded by my friends all night. I couldn't wait. I called the cab. I met them there.

A few lnights before, I shared a dream with the dream group I attended. I found others who believed in their dreams. Some think it's your conscience talking to you. Or your mind plays back what it saw through the day. I guess everyone dreams different. But me, I was different. I knew that. Charlie knew too because he saw and had premonitions like me. I started dreaming of brown eyes searching for me. Like they were looking for me. Joe, the instructor, told me I was looking for "myself" or best yet...my father. Isn't always easy to "interpret" what someone else sees? My eyes are green. I would get so mad at him. Why do you always say it's about my father! How could that be it? Then it gets into the what-ifs...I didn't believe in the what-ifs. Let's look at the symbols, which of course are important, too.

I told the dream class how I saw a dark figure of a man, like a shadow in my dreams. Like he was there for me, looking for me. I felt it, I felt "him." A masculine figure was in the middle of people. I couldn't see "him"; it was too dark, but I could feel him, like someone coming to you and you have this sense of security. Maybe that's why I dreamt that, because it was what I wanted. I couldn't see the others, either. But the only "shadow" I saw was "him." It was just a feeling I had in my soul, inside of me. I took a deep breath and got to exhale. Like comfort of love and comfort in the middle of your chest. It's like a feeling for me when I'm in church or catching my breath after running. I felt like God was sending me a messenger like before. Yet this was different. It was warm and I felt something so heavy inside me, but then again it felt enlightened—it felt like my soul had come alive and my love was coming to finally find me and hold me so I knew he was actually there. That's how real it felt. I could feel him. It would be an "energy." I could feel it. I could see myself reaching for him, too. I saw and felt this three times on three different nights in my dreams. I never dream of the same things, not even twice, but this was the third time.

In the Bible, there's an interpretation of Adam and Eve. God created woman for man. It makes sense. That's how you make babies! Now I'm not saying people who have relationships with the same sex is wrong. Everyone needs someone to love and be loved in return. But I know there is a God for what he has shown me so far. The Bible says woman and man he created. It explains that they were kicked out of heaven. Did they go back to heaven once they knew what was right? Is that how you get there? To heaven? By finding your real true love to go back "home"? Is that why there are so many souls and people on Earth? We haven't found our true love because we are so selfish, deceitful, and want to lie, the need to lie! Because we know what is bad and we know what is good. I wanted to be someone's Eve, someone's girl. I wanted to be the only girl for the only guy. I wanted to be really loved and know the love is real in return. I never felt that feeling with anyone else, that connection of man/woman love. I loved my friends and they say we have more than one soulmate. Because we are here so long? Is heaven actually being born into a better life here or does our soul go to heaven...eventually? With or without our true love soul mate?

You always hear about the story where a man and woman have been together for eighty years and die within a short period of time or right then and there together. Did they go to heaven? But my life never brought me to that. All through my life, I had options. But I think I have been punished also. Maybe from a past life.

So what do people do today to meet someone? I joined a dating website. Pretentious, as a friend would say. I had three dates lined up, one the next day. Guys would run up to me for dates. Literally! There were even the most handsome men who would tell me how beautiful I am. Some men that I could "run" with, be "in the scene." I didn't want false love. Even remembering my past. If a guy got closer to me, I would break up with him because I didn't want to hurt them. It was like something inside me was missing. I wanted the real thing.

But tonight, I just wanted to be with my friends. People who liked to live and celebrate life. They were so much fun and didn't go out of their way to hurt anybody. I really love them. They say when you don't expect it, it comes.

October 10, 2009 11:59P.M.

*A*manda was there with Bianca, and the gang. Angelica and her friend came later—it was a great night. I was drinking, having an excellent time with my friends. There was about 10 of us. Amanda had to go. I walked her outside, and we had one last cigarette. As we were talking, a group of motorcycle guys came up ...on Bell Blvd? I never seen so many at one time on this road. Amanda and I watched them line up—there were at least twenty of them. It was hard to miss them.

As they backed into their spots, all lined in a row, right across from us I told Amanda, "Wow—this is just like a dream I had." Because I saw the guy in the middle. I was looking at the "symbols." A guy got off his bike in the "middle." He was the only one wearing red. The others got off their bikes— they were all wearing black. I told my dream to Amanda.

I said, "Amanda, you see this?"

"I had a dream about someone in the middle, and look who is wearing a different color? The guy in the middle?" We laughed about it. She was probably just laughing with me because she thought I had too much to drink. I never spoke to her about my dreams. I hardly ever talked about them, but they were so strong I wanted them to know, maybe believe in me.

I kissed her goodbye, and I walked back into the club, where the rest of my friends were.

I found Bianca, where she was with the rest of the gang. The DJ was playing House Music, my favorite! I looked around and saw the motorcycle guy with the red vest. I had to go over and see who he was. I know I had that little smirk on my face.

I went up to him and asked, "Were you with the guys on the bikes from across the street?"

He shook his head no. I'm not an idiot, nor was I that drunk. I laughed and walked away, I knew it was him. As I walked away, I could "feel" something. I went to the dance floor and started dancing with my friends. Where I felt the safest. My feelings not feeling at all because the music was so loud. My eyes looked up, and I saw him. I saw this guy dancing with this girl. We made eye contact, only because I could feel him staring at me. But he was dancing with her.

I remember thinking, What is he doing with her? She was totally not his type, plus her bra straps were sticking out. He had this "aura" about him, like there was a glow around him. This classy look. He was smiling, looking at me while dancing with her. I didn't care. Maybe it was his friend, because he was definitely not into her. A great song came on, so I was dancing with myself, my hands in the air so free when I felt him come up behind me. I could smell him!

"This girl wants to dance with me, but I don't want to dance with her, I want to dance with you," right into my neck, so close to my ear. It was the most sexiest voice I ever heard in my life. And mind you, I have been around all accents. I turned around, and it was him. I could feel my heart pumping even over the loud bass from the music playing. I looked at him, at his eyes and knew I had to walk away. I went back over to my friends and looked back at him. There he was, in the center of my view. I only saw him. His hands were in his pockets, and he kinda shrugged like, here I am. He was "tall, dark, and handsome"! Now I wanted to know who he was. I walked over to him. I had to know where he was from. I loved finding out where people were from. Sometimes I even guessed right. My son's father was better at it than I was.

His eyes were dark, he felt mysterious, like he was from another world. I will never forget his eyes, they were the ones in my dream. I looked at my drink, stirring the straw (trying to be cute), and asked him,

What's your name? I asked

"Azir" he says

Azir...The letter A just like that silly quiz I took earlier "Where are you from?"

He replied, "I'm French."

"Do you know French?" I asked.

He replied, "Yes."

"Well, tell me something in French."

He said something.

"What did you say?"

He said, "I said you are beautiful."

My heart melted. I had this immediate appeal to him even more. Never has that ever happened before. Guys tell me I'm beautiful all the time. But when he said it to me, it was.... different. I looked up at him and said, "I just want to see something." I lifted on my toes and kissed him on the lips and opened my eyes. Wow! Never, Ever had I felt that. It's like I've kissed him before a thousand times. His kiss seemed so....familiar. He kissed me right back. Him I couldn't resist—I have no idea why. I felt like I felt in the dream in an instant. I didn't want to leave him, EVER. That's when my friends said they wanted to go.

They called over a cab as we all walked out and asked, "Kelly, how are you getting home?" I said, "I'll be fine," as I was holding his hand (which, by the way, fit perfectly). I could hear Angelica in her high- pitched tone, "No, she doesn't know him, we can't leave her with him." I closed the cab door, laughing. I hear Bianca saying, "She's fine!" They didn't understand. But my friend Bianca knew I would be fine. We smiled at each other, then the cab took off.

When I first met Bianca we both knew we would be friends forever. It's strange because I didn't meet her until just recently and we lived down the road from each other and went to the same school when we were younger. Like God doesn't put people into your life until certain times and reasons.

I always lived life this way, never knowing, just going with what I "felt." I wanted to go with him and he wanted me to go with him too. Isn't that the way we are supposed to go, our path? Are our lives written already, or do we make them up as we go along?

We walked into this restaurant that was still opened at 1 A.M. There was a family, I would say of eight people. We walked in, and he ordered us drinks at the tiny bar in the back of the restaurant. There was a band playing Mediterranean music. We were talking—exchanging information.

"Can I ask you a question?" Thinking about that silly little quiz from this morning. "Sure", he replied

I asked, "When is your birthday?"

"The beginning of May, when is yours?"

He said he was a flight attendant. He made a remark about the beauty mark on my upper lip and said it was perfect kissing, bringing his fingers to his lips like an Italian guy. I was thinking about him being a flight attendant, saying, "You must have seen so many sunsets and the beautiful world." He stopped—getting up, he said, "This is what's beautiful." He walked over to the three-year-old spinning on the dance floor. She was wearing a white dress. He spun her around. It was like a fantasy, a dream, the music, the white dress, the beautiful family having dinner together, plus my one too many drinks. While he was dancing with her, I noticed a girl about seven, sitting there, sulking. Sitting there sulking while the pretty younger sister got all the attention because she was laughing and having fun. I walked over to her, not caring what the family would say. They said she was being punished for being mean to her little sister. I sat next to her and asked her, "Are you a princess?" She nodded yes. I said, "Well, I'm a princess, too." She looked up at me. I remember me telling her, "princesses are supposed to be good and kind, especially to their sisters. Plus little sister is dancing with my guy." She giggled, got up, hugged, and danced with her sister. The family responded with smiles and took pictures, and I got to dance with him. We were dancing until the band closed. It might have been only twenty minutes but felt like we were there for hours. Talking about the world moving slowly. He said he wanted me to stay with him. I didn't want to leave him still. We were walking down Bell Blvd. While walking I told him things I never told anybody! I pulled him closer, saying, "I never want to leave you." I felt like myself next to him. Like I knew him forever. He stopped and kissed me. We kept walking and of course, being a girl, I complained, "It's so far!" He laughed and grabbed my hand. I remember kissing and laughing with him all the way there. As we were walking, I remembered thinking, "This feels so amazing!" I loved listening to his voice. Maybe it was the feeling of the mysteriousness (or the alcohol, which would eventually wear off), not knowing who he was, but I didn't care—it felt, no words could describe it. Unbelievable to be with him, and I was so comfortable, in a strange way. Like I've known him before yet I never met anyone like him. Like this is where I'm supposed to be at this moment. We arrived at the hotel and went into the room. I remember us kissing and me being confident.

Too much to drink!

I woke up with him saying, "Let's go, time to get up," He tapped my leg and walked into the bathroom.

I said, "I'll call a cab."

He replied, "No, we are going to Astoria to watch the soccer game."

"I'm going with you?"

"Of course!" he said. "I have a driver that is taking us there"

A few more hours with him. This guy who I knew nothing about but wanted nothing more to be next to him. We go down to the lobby. Azir met his driver and made me coffee before we left. He opened the back door for me to get in. Then we were on our way. I had to stop at my place first so I could change. He came up with me and walked around my apartment almost inspecting looking around while I got ready. Of course I had dishes in the sink. We go back into the van and headed for Astoria. As for the driver? He spoke Arabic, a language I didn't understand. I've been around "foreigners" all my life. It felt like Azir was saying, "No, she's okay," in that laidback way. The driver showed me a picture of what would be his daughter. Nothing amazing, I thought, and passed it back to the front but not in my sincere tone, saying she was beautiful. I didn't care too much for the driver. I was thinking to myself looking at Azir from behind, "What am I doing here?" The coffee was terrible but needed after a hangover. We arrived, got out, and the driver took off. It was a cold day for October around here. "I have no money," I said as we were passing my brand bank. He pulled me gently. "You don't need money." "But I have no cigarettes." He took his out for me. I smiled. How could I not? He was prepared! We went to an opened food place and sat down. I really didn't want to eat but did. I looked at his face, big brown eyes, his cheeks and jawline, the outline of his lips, how perfect. He looked right at me and winked...friggin' professional, I thought, and continued to eat. I did blush a little. We went to another place to watch the game. A hookah lounge. I was the only woman in there. But I didn't feel uncomfortable. He ordered a hookah and some drinks for us. Never using a lamp before, he laughed at the way I used it and showed me how to do it. Loved the smell. As soon as I walked in, that too seemed so familiar. He knew what team to root for. I loved the way he held my hand, the way he looked at me. I felt...something in me that I never felt before. While he was holding my hand, my head was on his shoulder, the driver walked in. The driver kept looking at our hands up at Azir, then back down again in disbelief almost over and over again. I lifted my head off his shoulder. Azir didn't notice at first. I tapped his hand with my thumb. He looked at me, then up at the driver. Waived hello with his other hand and continued to watch the game. I felt really uncomfortable with the way the driver was looking, so I started to pull back my hand but he held on to it like he wanted the driver to see it more...time to go. Game over.

We went back to the hotel. Went in the room, settled down, and he lit a cigarette for me and himself. As I took a drag, he came in to kiss me. No one ever did that, I thought, as I was laughing 'cause it seemed so typical, a girl and guy in a hotel room, but his lips made me kiss him right back and I loved kissing him, smoke and all. To me it was the hottest thing. Kissing him with smoke coming out of my mouth.

As he drew the curtains to sleep, I remember him coming into bed and being perfectly next to me. As I melted into him, I thought "How could I do this with just some guy". As I started to relax, he must have thought I was sleeping. He pulled his hand out from under my head really gently. It was actually very sweet. Then he turned over and he fell asleep, As I looked at him, his back was facing me. His skin was golden brown, so perfect, as I slid my finger down his back. Then I thought, "Did he not want to hold me? Did he have someone else from his country and now felt guilty, or was he used to sleeping alone?" Oh, girls' heads never stop thinking. I kissed his back so I could feel my lips on his skin. I slide my hand in between his arm and hip to feel him closer to me. He didn't respond to grab my hand, so I started pulling back. He put his elbow into my arm. Asking me to leave it there without words. I did. I stayed there. I always felt like I was next to him. Like the missing puzzle. Then I dozed off.

His "afternoon" alarm went off. It was time for him to leave. As I was getting myself together he asked if I had international calling. I didn't. He just got out of the shower wearing purple heart underwear...really? Purple hearts on a guy? He wasn't gay! Purple is my favorite color. I laughed a little like my little angels were laughing at me, almost like another sign. Sounds silly but I don't think so. He was putting his shirt on.

"Will I see you again?" I asked.

"Yes," he said, stopping and kissing me.

I called and the representative asked where I would be calling.

"Where are you from again?"

"Kuwait," he says. That's right. Right then and there, all alarms must have been going off. An American girl's connecting with a guy from Kuwait? I thought of Operation Desert Storm. All our military and trucks on the shores of Kuwait. Picturing the news articles in my head from years ago. We tried to call each other and even tried to send emails. It wasn't working right then. He put his left leg up on the bed right next to me and was checking my phone to see what the issue was. While he was looking through my phone, I looked at his long leg, then up at him. He was absolutely perfect. He continued to get ready.

He stopped, "You have no money!"

"I'll be fine," I said.

He went into his pocket, took out a $50, $5, $1 bills. He gave me the $50 without hesitation. "No, it's ok," I said, looking at him. "I'll stop at the bank." But he gave me this look, so I took it. Then he says, "You have no cigarettes," taking a pack out of his luggage. He thought of me and being without. It was refreshing for someone to "take care of me." Like he really cared if I didn't have. Even every door he held open for me. He was a gentleman, and it was really nice of him.

The cab was called, and as we were saying goodbye I looked at his badge. Only because it was sticking me in the face while we hugged each other goodbye. I saw his picture. Usually I would check out the address, but his face. The darkness in his eyes, that straightforward hard look. Was that him? They didn't look the same, his eyes. Reminded me of the eyes of the men that knocked down "my twin towers". He must have seen the look on my face because he took his hand and put it under my chin. Gently lifted my chin to look "at him." Both of his thumbs were on my cheeks as he had his fingers in my hair. He kissed the side of my nose, my cheek, then my lips. When our lips met and I melted all over again. Like a thousand times, I thought to myself. Like a thousand times. As I went to the elevator, he stood by the door, as elevator opened, he closed the door to his room. Of course, a coworker of his was right there in front of me. I walked in and he was more than inclined to press the button and to make sure I "got out okay," letting me go first. Thank you. I got into the taxi and thought, "Great! Me leaving a hotel in a cab...." Did I feel like a prostitute or what...but then I thought about him and knew I wasn't. I loved the way he made me feel. He made me feel like a girl.

Leaving in the cab was like a movie, like lovers parting at the end. They say not to look back, but I did. I saw the second-floor room, where we were with the light on. If I didn't see him ever again, I wouldn't care because I knew he would be a part of me forever. I got home, no one was there, but for some reason I didn't feel lonely. I knew now that there was this feeling in me. Was this Love? This feeling I had in me? I just met him, can't be. It was like nothing I had felt before. Like I found something special from throughout this whole world! But like I said, if I didn't see him ever again he could never hurt me because I now have this fantasy, this dream I knew was true and real. I went back to Bell Blvd to get dinner. Anything you want. Italian is good. I walked in and saw a family I knew having dinner. I kissed them and ordered my dinner to go.

A few days later on Wednesday, I had a dream he read my email and was smiling. It was like he was right next to me, smiling down right next to me to kiss me again. I could feel him, and he wasn't even next to me. He was happy, I felt it, and I was happy when I woke up. I haven't heard from him. Like I said if I never heard from him again I have this memory that I was content with.

That Friday he called me just as I was in a rush as usual. It was girl's bingo night. I had to stop to get the girls' bingo gift then pick up Bianca. As I was in the store a call came into my cell. A number I didn't recognize—international? I pick up.

"Hello?"

"Hi, do you know who this is?" he asked.

"Of course" I said

"I'm with some friends in London...I'm sick, I'm sick, I can't stop thinking of you." I told him I felt the same way. I remembered the dream from the other night. I told him I dreamt of him. He asked if he was happy in the dream. I told him yes, it was true. I could see, feel him smile through the phone. I could "hear his smile" through the line, like he was right next to me in my dream. I had to go. I was running late. I was so happy to hear from him. He asked me to come meet him in his country, Tunisia. No way could I go there. Another country to meet him? Especially by myself to Africa? I told him I really wanted to but knew it would be impossible. The money, time, leaving my son? How could I? I just met him and I'm going to meet him on the other side of the world?

"Think about it." He says and we said goodbye.

After we got to the girls' house, settled in, got our drinks, I went out for a cigarette. The stars never seemed so bright, the world seemed so small, but most of all, my heart was happy. This feeling in me was unexplainable. I felt like he "felt" me. Was it because I dreamt of him? Was it because he made me smile just thinking of him? Did he really feel the same way about me?

I called him back the next day.

"I love the sound of your voice", I told him

I love your.....all of you! He says

 Then he says, "I trust you."

"You trust me?" I asked.

"Yes," he replied. "Please come with me and spend time with me in my country. I want to be there with you."

So I start looking online about Tunisia. They are most friendly of the Arab nations with the United States. Loved the internet. I can find anything on there! My dreams were coming to me again. So strong one right after another. I was seeing the next day again. One night I had a dream that I'm on a bus.

11/2/09: I dreamt of a bus pulling into a cobblestone driveway. The driveway went down, so you had to go in on the left side. There was a wedding about to take place because you could smell the flowers and hear the church bells in the bacground. I walked into the room on the right. You could see the driveway from the window. I picked up to smell the flowers, then woke up. All the other dreams came true. Except this one.

I was also dreaming of art, pictures, moments, conversations. I guess because I was looking up Tunisia. So much history and art. She was beautiful country. No wonder he loved his hometown. But then again, I think everyone loves where they come from.

I get a call from him the next day. He's in London again and he says go to the computer and order my ticket to Tunisia. I finally agreed to meet him. I place the order, I'm leaving next week.

 The next day I tell my friends I'm going to Tunisia!

"Where is that?" one asks.

"It's northern Africa", I replied.

She did not like that. "No way! No way are you going there! Nope, no way!"

"Are you serious?" I asked, laughing. She tried to yell at me, but her yelling was just a slight whisper—I appreciated the way she cared.

"Do you know what they would do to you?"

"No…I will be with Azir," I told her.

"Kelly! You don't even know him and you're going to meet him halfway across the world? They have human smuggling and prostitution rings!"

I didn't care, I told her, thinking I never felt this way and I'm going to go with what I felt, to be with him. She was right though, I didn't know him at all.

Turns out the next day is a completely different story. I wasn't going. He said his cousin died and he wouldn't be in Tunisia. Maybe that explained the white sand dream I had. I couldn't go there now, that I knew. He is the one who had to get everything together. I told him I would be here for him if he needed me or to have someone to talk. I felt like a stupid girl. He just invited you, then uninvited you!? I tried to believe what he told me. Why would he lie about that? I tried to believe it. I actually cried that night. Then I realized I had a plane ticket with nowhere to go. It had to be rebooked or the money would be lost. So I searched online for other places. I love the saying "Life isn't about waiting for the storm to pass; it's about learning to dance in the rain." Well, I wasn't going to sit there and cry over some guy who didn't care. I had to block my feelings or at least try too.

I searched for destinations the airline went to. Not the Caribbean, the airline didn't go there. I decided to go to Rome. No lying on the sand by a pool and the ocean. But Rome did have a history there with the columns, statues, cobblestone roads, and sidewalks all like I saw in my dreams. The Trevi Fountain, I thought of Neptune, the Coliseum, the ancient ruins where Cleopatra and Marc Anthony walked. Perfect!

While scrolling down looking for places to stay, one struck my eye. It was the one just like my dream. I clicked on the link, just like the dream with the driveway, where the door was, exactly the same with flowers all around and the cobblestone driveway. It was like the more I believed in my dreams, the more they would come true.

There was this dream I told about to my dream class, I was with God. There were columns knocked down. He was the almighty. He was throwing down thunderbolts toward the east, trying to protect me from someone. But who? Charlie from the dream group called it Divine Intervention. I believed that. How could science do this? I really could see the events happening the next day. Sometimes they weren't in order. That's what was so confusing also. This was something more, something real. I would dream of shooting stars only to see the next morning on the internet that there was a meteor shower that night. Then there was one where a tornado ripped through the south. How could this not be something more than the people in this world? All those stories of ancient aliens, prophecies, who knew what was real? There really was something more. Years ago the prophets, even Nostradamus, had to "hide"; otherwise, they would be considered witches and be burned at stake. He held up a book that was blank. Like he didn't know the future anymore. But now my dreams, the way I was, it wasn't like before where if they happened and I just went on. This time it intrigued me more. I wanted to know why. And why little ole me?

12/02/2009

*I*was in Italy. You would think something major would happen here. Maybe I drew myself there on my own from my own subconscious. Isn't that what you're supposed to think? It was like I imagined. Beautiful, I could feel the history in my soul. At one point, I did stop at a payphone. I had his number in my pocket, ready to call him. My hand was on the paper with his number on it. Then I stopped myself. I pulled out my hand and left the number in my pocket. "Kelly, why are you calling him? He didn't even care to reply back to you, knowing you would be so close." But then maybe his cousin really did die. I felt sad and disappointed in myself, my feelings, what I thought I felt, and even what I saw. I went to the ruins. I tried to make the best of it, how could I not, I thought, and continued on. I walked around Rome. I looked for signs and saw them all. Even the street names had my son's and best friend's names on them. The little things. I met some beautiful people while there. A lot of people speak English in Italy. There was a restaurant I went to, and it felt like home. The people there seemed so familiar. I felt comfortable being there. Even hanging out hours after the restaurant closed. I tried to explain to the owner why I came here. "Talk slower," he says.

I got around pretty good by myself in another country. I did find someone safe to spend time with while there. The next day I sat to have a glass of wine, overlooking the river that ran in front of Castle D'Angelo. I found a little restaurant not too far from the Trevi Fountain. There was Christmas ornaments and lightbulbs hanging from one side of the alleyway to the other across. The woman who owned it was from Brazil. Really? From Brazil you are here? And she spoke English! She was very sweet and had a warm smile. She was tall and had the looks of a supermodel. You could tell she was a good person. As she came out and placed the glass on the table, I notice the number of the building I was sitting in front of. 28 was the number carved in stone, again like a recent dream. I was supposed to be here but again, why? I see this "Italian Man" standing in the alleyway, smiling at me. "Look in your book, Kelly," I laughed to myself. He didn't come over, maybe because I looked away. He even had the pink sweater wrapped around his shoulders. Je ne sais quoi. I wasn't looking for a one-night stand again.

I felt like God was putting me on the right path but wouldn't tell me why. I went to the fountain and placed all my friends' coins in them. Even my tarot cards told me I'm not supposed to know. The high priestess. But how can I get these sightings and not want to know WHY? It was only when God wanted me to know, I guess. All I knew was I was here because of some guy whom I thought was different from the rest. Then I laughed at myself for believing that. So naive but I couldn't let him go. It's like a dream you will always remember. There was just something about him that made my heart pound. The dreams, the way he made me feel, and the presence of God all together, I didn't know what to think. I would have been fine with just the memory of being with him. Why did he have to call me after and make me feel these things? I couldn't wait to get home, my comfort zone, after a few days. I was even stopped, and my luggage was checked at the airport after the flight. I just wanted to get home, and I couldn't get out of the airport! Why me? Did I look like a terrorist? There were plenty of others who should have been looked at, but me? Finally I'm out and my friends are waiting for me, we went out for dinner. Hibachi. I felt better to be home and with them, laughing and catching up.

I got home and back to life. I called him two days later. I knew I shouldn't have, he picked up. He sounded sick, like he was crying, sad. He said he was ill and that's why he sounded that way. Something didn't seem right. He said he was coming in on December 20th and he would contact me. I had hope once again and happiness in my heart.

Well, the 20th came and no word from him. I must have checked my email a hundred times but nothing. I went to sleep and realized maybe everyone was right. Bianca and my friend Mike from upstate always said forget him, he's not coming back. He was just a passing phase that I had to get out of. What they didn't realize is I don't get stuck like this. It's like he had total control of me and I didn't want him to. The next morning I got up, made coffee, and started the computer as I do every morning to check new emails. There were two from him that he sent late last night. I've never received one from him before. I only spoke to him on the phone. It said he was here to see me and he missed me.

"Baby, I'm in New York. I'm waiting for you. Reply back because I can't receive calls and I don't have credit in my phone, Your baby, Azir, kisses."

Then he gave me the address of the hotel with his room number. "I miss you and I came here to see you."

"You came to see me? I thought you were here all the time," I thought to myself. "And no credit in your phone? Why?" But I called him anyway at the hotel, and he answered. I had this draw to him.

"How come you didn't call me sooner?" he asked.

"Because I didn't check my emails until the morning."

He said he would have gotten in touch with me sooner, but because of the snow and the bus drivers were on strike again he got to the hotel late. "Come now." Like a magnet, I said okay. I took a shower, thank God I cleaned the day before, I thought to myself as I left. I get to the hotel, the drive wasn't too bad but there was a lot of snow. I see the other flight attendants in the lobby.

I went in the elevator, got out, and found the room. I knocked on the door. My heart was beating so fast. What if he was different this time, what if all he thought of me had gone? What if he wasn't what I remembered? I watched as the handle on the door slowly turned down and the door slowly opened. I didn't see him until I stepped into the dark room. It smelled like smoke and cologne. Our eyes met, we both smiled, and that's the last thing I knew, my lips were on his and it happened so fast...like a magnet. We stood there kissing for what felt like forever. It was a moment I knew I would always remember, like standing in time. My body couldn't move, his didn't move, either. We were just there kissing, no hot "touch me all over" type of kiss, but it was passion. It felt like he was talking to me in it, saying, I've missed you, I felt nothing else. I didn't know where I was, I felt lost in time, like there was no such thing as time and how perfect it felt to be near him again. I felt that. I never felt anything like that ever. I separated my lips from his and whispered, "I missed you so much," and put my head on his shoulder. He put his hand on my head and held me into him. "No talking," he said, and took a deep sigh of relief as he was still holding me into him and kissed my head. I dropped my purse on the floor. It was still in my hand this whole time. I told you I couldn't move, not even to drop my purse or put it on anything! I didn't even realize it was still in my hand. Eventually I did, and that's when he bent down, picked it up, and put it on the dresser. He walked over to me, and as he sat on the bed, I told him, "I didn't think you were real, I thought I would never see you again." He didn't know I dreamt of this feeling of him before I met him. He replied, "Not in this lifetime." I pushed him back on the bed and went in to kiss him. Kissing we rolled over so perfectly, he kissed my arm all the way down and back up again. He was perfect in every way.

As we were lying on the bed, it felt like a cloud, he was on one side and I was on the other. I loved the way the white sheets contrasted with his skin, his golden color. He still had that glow. I opened my eyes to see his were closed, then he opened them, looking right at me. We both smiled, and I closed mine. I could hear his open again like butterfly kisses. I told him, "This whole time we were apart, you're all the way over." We met in the middle, and being in his arms I felt safe and warm, like I was floating on a cold winter day. Again like this is where I'm supposed to be at this very moment. He fell asleep. When he awoke, he wanted something to eat, and him staying until the next day he would come back with me. "I'm all yours," he said. "I want to go to this place that has the best hummus, it's Mediterranean, I think you will like it."

"What do you want?" he asked.

"Hummus, you know, chickpeas," he laughed and said it a little different. "That's what I said," laughing, he smiled.

"They make that in Lebanon."

"You should have met me in Italy," I said.

He replied, "Why you met someone while you were there? Didn't you?" And looked right at me. How did he know that? I met someone there, but I didn't want to be with him, I thought but didn't say it out loud. I replied, "I meet people all the time." The place was closed so we headed to Queens. We went to an Italian restaurant I went to a few times with my friends. There was a little old couple across the way from me and him. It was cute, but they weren't talking to each other, just eating. He looked over at them, too. He started to tell me things about himself. Little things. He ate his bread with a fork and knife and told me about his mother. I could see her, a beautiful, classy lady, and what he liked to eat. It's funny because of all the things I wanted to know about him I didn't think to ask. Like how he grew up. I didn't have to, though, because we were together and we would eventually know everything soon enough, anyway. Right? The owner came in, saw me, and said, "Hi, sweetie," then looked at him and said hello. I introduced them. They shook hands, and the owner walked away and dimmed the lights. It was perfect. Time to go, we made a few stops on the way and arrived at my place. I opened my door, he stepped in, and as I went to lock it, he already did and pushed in the door, locking it. The way he did it kind of shocked me, the way he knew which lock it was and how to turn it and push it in. He came in and noticed some things were moved around. "Well, I had to make room for the Christmas tree from the last time you were here and get ready for Christmas." We watched a few movies.

We made drinks and smoked. We kissed and had our clothes off. I loved him. Right until I went back in to kiss him and had the vision of a demon. I tensed up but continued on. Was he a demon, or was it something inside me telling me not to feel, not to love? I felt uncomfortable but the need to have him, to want him. I still loved him even though this is the 2nd time I'm seeing him. I wanted more of him even though he may be evil. But what if he wasn't? My mind again running wild thinking too much. I woke up late, maybe on purpose and called in sick to work. He was sleeping so I went to the store to get us something to eat. I came back he was still in my bed. He woke, we ate, and then it was time to go. I had to drop him back at the hotel and it was already later than we should have left. As we were leaving, I locked my door, then was about to start going down the stairs, he grabbed me and kissed me so hard, so long. It was like a goodbye kiss. What if it wasn't? I kissed him right back. "Hold on to the banister, Kelly," I thought since I felt a little "floaty" going down the steps. As he was going down, I told him, "I miss you already." He stop, turned around, kissed me again on the lips and replied, "Me too." Of course, there's a lot of traffic and time surely wasn't moving slowly. I remembering him staring at me. I couldn't look back because I had to pay attention to the road. Maybe he was staring, like how I could drive like that? I'm from New York! He said he will be in on Christmas

Eve. He played with the radio, looking for my favorite song at that time. I told him to call me when he came in. We pull up to the hotel, I put my car in park. He took my hand and kissed it.

I asked him "I'll talk to you in a few days when you're back?" as he was getting out of the car.

"It's all in God's hands." He said. Kissed my hand again and told me to be safe, and I wished him safety as well. He closed the car door and walked to the hotel. I thought it was strange the way he said that, considering the way he kissed me on my steps the way he did. There was that feeling of good-bye again. I didn't have that secure feeling anymore, but I knew I still had these strong feelings for him, about him. I didn't hear from him Christmas Eve.

There's a saying: "Some lives stretch across the sands of time, that they are connected by an ancient calling that echoes through the ages."

When I think of that saying, I think of the past, present, and future calling out for help. So many people have lost a loved one due to war since the beginning of time humans were "kicked out of heaven." War for land. War to see who the best is? No one wins, actually. We lose something, someone. Do we pray for faith or hope?

I always wondered why some fall in love very early and have found their "one" or why one person is born rich and another poor. Or why people "reunite" when they are older. Did they follow/not follow the 10 Commandments and have to come back into a different status? Is that why there are so many people/souls who are still on "earth"? Like we haven't proven our trueness, our goodness, our true love to go up to heaven. Are we in heaven now? But then why do children die? What did they do?

January 2010

*G*eat New Year's Eve party with my friends! I saw so many people I knew. Even my neighbor that I was allowed to go out with once a month when I was with my son's father. And had to be home by 12 A.M.!

I tried to call him. Either he didn't pick up or his phone was out of range. This was my worse month ever in business. I was a top sales person in my department. I was so sad. I couldn't concentrate. Just the thought of him made my eyes tear up. What the hell was wrong with me! I wasn't like this. I'm a strong girl. My upbringing made it easy for me to cut off feelings just like that. If someone didn't want to be in my life or they didn't want me to be in theirs, you just cut it off. Sometimes you will be sad or have similar feelings, but you move on. I couldn't move on from this. I couldn't sleep because I didn't want to see him in my dreams. I kept dreaming about him like he was there but I couldn't touch him. The feeling was too strong. It was my worse production month ever! One day I couldn't even go to work. My eyes were so puffy from crying, it was embarrassing. One morning after I called in "sick," I was on my sofa, still crying. Tissues to wipe the tears.

I HEARD THAT VOICE AGAIN!

"How do you feel?"

Loud and clear! The same voice I heard a week before my grandmother died. Was it God? Why does he talk to me?

I literally yelled back so loud I didn't care if the neighbors heard me, "**It doesn't feel good!** Okay!? I'm sorry! What did I do?" The tears rolled down my face. I literally yelled out back to him...my father.

I laid back down on the couch and closed my eyes. I tried to open them but only that they are flooded with tears. When I closed them, I could see ancient markings and carvings in a stone wall. Then I thought of what I did. I tried to drink him away, tried to man him away. Nothing worked. I wasn't perfect, but other people have done so much worse than what "I did." Then I thought if I really loved him I wouldn't have to be with anyone else. But if he really loved me then I wouldn't feel this way.

Around that time I had a dream of him where he was about to be killed in front of a crowd on a platform. It felt like the 1800's. Two men covered up wearing all black walked him out, his hands tied behind his back. Azir was wearing beige pants and a white collar shirt. They made him get on his knees. The "man" wearing all black pulled out his knife. He was going to kill him. I was off to the side being held back, screaming, "No! No! Don't kill him! He's innocent! He didn't do anything wrong!" I wanted to run and save him. Then I woke up. Did that happen in our past life? Maybe it was me telling myself to cut him out of my life because I knew I had to.

I couldn't be like this anymore. My body was starting to hurt, was I depressed? No way, not me. What's the next step? Go on medication? Reminded me of when I was with my son's father and took pills for "my depression." It was because I was unhappy, sad. To me the sadness was making me sick. There was nothing else wrong with me. Feel sorrier for myself that my heart actually broke like the Queen of Hearts. They say she actually died of a broken heart. My dreams were so confusing.

Some people don't even get to feel or see these things in a lifetime. I felt lucky, but then I felt loss. I read the Bible a lot trying to find meaning I hung out with my friends. I went back to being happy again. I felt better. Even in my pictures, I looked happier. But he was always in the back of my mind. Especially seeing the airplanes flying to JFK. They were all around me. By my job with JFK, by my house with LaGuardia. Thinking of the dreams I would see of him at his airport. Every song, every movie I watched had airplanes in it. Even my brother, agreed. He saw it.

Soon after that I started calling him again. Sometimes he answered. Then he would call me from London, France, Bangkok, Kuwait. He always asked about my son and if I was okay. Then I stopped hearing from him again.

I think I was still pretty lucky, though. I got to feel what that was like, love. A real, true connection in this world. But this was more than that. I couldn't describe. I always wondered if he was okay and happy. Still to this day. I didn't want this connection to him, but I couldn't help it.

There was so much fighting going on around the world. Suicide bombings in the Middle East. Anyone is scared if that's going to happen anywhere. Would he be caught up in it one day since he is all over the world? Was he apart of it? Why would people do this? Ruin their town or want to kill people. Someone, somewhere will lose someone they love. Is that God's will? I don't think so.

I always thought if they are "that religious" that God told them this is the right thing to do. There's no way! Only God decides that. Maybe it's like the Greek mythology where there is a Hades on the side for hate and God/Zeus is the side of Love. The one true God!

April, 2010

I was still going to dream class. I still dreamt of my friends, the places we would go to. There was this dream I had that I was Upstate with my friends. I see three women. The one in the middle had blonde hair with a pixie cut. The three women were holding three sparklers each as we were sitting around a bonfire.

My son was doing terrible at school. I had a dream of a pencil, a hairspray cap, and this brown oval object all on a small table. The class interpreted the pencil as my son not doing well at school and the cap was to put a lid on it. I could accept that. But this was a vision. My dreams were so strong once again. Some were coming true and some weren't. I was driving my coworker home, and she mentioned she saw a psychic who was so on point. Wow, perfect timing and the perfect person to see! I immediately wrote down her number and called her right away. I gave her my first name only and made the appointment that would be in her house. I tried to look her up online. Nothing.

I arrived at the appointment and as soon as I opened the door I looked right at her. She was one of the 3 women in the recent dream I had. She was the blonde woman holding a set of the three sparklers. I laughed a little. She immediately said,

"Who is the letter 'A' and why aren't you sleeping?"

"That's why I'm here!"

"Sit down and shuffle the cards. Do you have a picture of him?"

She runs the cards.

"Ghessezz, this guy is all over the place. I see soccer, the number ten (I met him on October 10th), does he stare at you? I can see him staring at you." I thought of when we first met and driving with him in the car. I told her he was a flight attendant. That explains the all over the place. "Do you believe in past lives? Where does the letter 'M' come from?"

"That's his first name," I replied.

"You guys have had a past life together. You have a very strong connection to him, this I think is the strongest I ever seen. When you met him was it like love at first sight, like an instant connection, right? He thinks about you a lot"

That's exactly what I felt. She could feel it. She saw it. She said, "He has a lot of money and there's a woman in his life whom he is very close to, not romantic kind like a girlfriend." I remember him saying he stayed with his sister. I didn't care about the money part. Then she says, "You were supposed to go see him and someone died. Definitely a past life, and you both love each other but something else is going on. You guys are going to be together for a long time but you won't "be together". You can't be together. Good News is that you're getting married in the fall." That didn't make any sense to me. " It's not going to work out. He doesn't like your lifestyle." She said Azir is going to come back and sees a lot of computer activity." Did she see all those embarrassing emails I sent confessing my love to him? I could feel the heat in my face. Maybe it was me that pushed him away. At least he knew how I felt.

"Do you have a little girl?" Confused, I said no. She was right about everything else. She also said, "He is going to meet your son. And I see a little girl with you." We spoke about other things, which she was also correct about. She told me to continue what I was doing and it will be successful. I thought she was referring to the violin classes I signed up for. She told me I have a very strong gift, a psychic gift.

I said, "Yes, I can dream."

"You've had it since you were little. Did you ever tell him you had a dream about him? He's afraid of that."

Before I left, she stopped me and says, "It feels like electricity, doesn't it?" I said yes and walked out. That was the feeling in me and I didn't know how to stop it.

I couldn't stop the tears from falling out as I walked to my car. . That's exactly how I felt. Electricity, like this very spiritual connection. Finally the feeling was understood. Now who is this guy I'm supposed to marry? And why can't I be with Azir?

I kept myself busy. One night my girlfriend and I went out for a few drinks. When I got home I wanted to talk to him so I called him. I haven't spoken to him in so long! Will he pick up? He picked up. "Don't you know who I am? I can have any guy I want and you don't want me. Maybe I want you more because I can't have you." He made me repeat that.

"It's my family, I told you already." I remember him telling me about how his family wanted him to marry someone.

"Well, I don't care" I told him. "You don't call me. What is wrong with you? Why can't I just see you?"

Laughing he said, "Okay, okay, wait for me. Wait for me," he says

. A few weeks go by and I haven't heard from Azir. He disappeared again. His phone was out of range. I felt like I was slipping back into that sadness stage I was in, again! Now I realized he really doesn't want to hear from me anymore. I get a call from Brian. He was a Turkish guy I met in a club a few months back. Very young, but he was mature for his age and probably what I needed right now. I actually went up to him. I remember the day I met him. He was standing there right in the middle of the club with no one around him. Shoulder length hair, a sports jacket with jeans, hand on his hip. He was confidant! I went right over to him.

"Hi, I'm Kelly. Who are you?" I asked. He smiled and then we went from there. We definitely liked each other.

We would smoke and drink stay up for hours. I always loved talking to him. He was a great guy. From a good family with morals. We talked about religion, he was Muslim. We talked about the world, everything! Turkey was divided among themselves because of trade and how the government was deciding how the people should live. He was proud to be on the side he was on since the East and West were divided. When spouses would want to divorce, the family comes together. Here it's so easy to let it go.

I tried to call Azir, but he never called back. Why should I wait for someone who hasn't proven he cares about me? So I hung out with Brian.

A few days after seeing Brian, I see a post on social media from someone. It said, "Can you believe this guy asks a girl to wait for him since she says she loves him and he says he's busy and wait, minutes later she was with some other guy? What a whore." I immediately thought of myself. How

41

could this club guy and my guy be linked? But Azir wasn't calling me back. Why should I wait for someone who didn't show any interest? And maybe this post wasn't about me because how could this guy know my guy? But it is a small world.

May 1, 2010

News alert. Someone tried to set off a bomb in Manhattan, in Times Square. Why are people doing this? Why would they want to blow us up and wasn't 9/11 enough? You hear all the time about suicide bombers all over the world doing this. As you already know, I think only God should take your life. Who is one person to decide if you should live or not? I remembered learning in school that when Japanese suicide bombers do "their mission," they are rewarded in a past life. Some think they will get seventy-two virgins. I think you will but you will never be able to "have" them. They are virgins and will always stay that way. Be careful what you ask for. Then I thought of how you should ask God for things. I think if you truly want something, you can have it. Was I not sincere enough and that's why Azir left or that's why he can't be in my life? Our feelings and times change so much, it's hard to truly and sincerely decide what you want. So maybe God doesn't give it to you.

End of May, 2010

*A*friend calls me over, "Read this, Kelly." It was an article in the news-paper after the Times Square incident. It named an airline, his airline, that had an unauthorized passenger in October and December 2009. It also stated how "they" send information back over to whomever wants it. Small packages. I read it about five times. It wasn't a very big article. He saw the hurt in my face, eyes tearing up and my hand shaking. He put his hand on mine.

"They are trained to do this, Kelly." He knew of the 2 times I saw Azir aka the flight attendant.

"No, he was different." I told him

My tears welled in my eyes. How to go back to life, to work, and con-centrate. Was he a terrorist? After reading that article remembering he carried a bag from his driver, thinking of the times he disappeared and why he doesn't want to see me if he said he was here several times a month. I called him and he answered.

"How are you? I'm surprised you picked up but I took a chance"

"I'm doing okay, I'm here" he says.

I got right to the point. I asked him straight out.

"Are you a terrorist?"

"What? No!" he said. He sounded hurt.

"There's that training," I thought. But what if he wasn't and I'm making a big mistake?

"How could you say something like that to me?"

"Well, you carried that package for your 'driver.'" He did say he would bring it to the drivers daughter. I remembered him looking through it, though. There was nothing I saw that I would think to be a threat to my country! We were actually laughing about the things he was sending her. He said he had to go and I will hear from him soon.

Maybe he was a sincere traveler looking for love, is just a worldwide spoiled brat "lover," or maybe he really is a terrorist.

Memorial Day weekend, May 2010

I drove Upstate to meet my friends in a house they rented. There's always over ten people. When I got there, everyone was out ATV-ing, so no one was at the house. I found the key where Bianca said she left it. I put my stuff down since I didn't know what room I would be in. I made myself a drink. Looked around, it was so beautiful. There even was a little stream running through the trees. There were purple flowers growing wild. Like in the songs of my America with purple mountain majesties. I felt like God was hugging me with all this beauty.

I was about to sit down in the lounge chair when something caught my eye. It was a pencil, a spray can cap, and a melted beer bottle all on a little table. It was exactly like the dream I had a few months ago. That vision. I dropped my cigarette into the ashtray, grabbed my camera, and took a picture. I tried to call a girl from dream class and left a message. I have to say I was a little shaken up. That's when I heard them coming. The dirt kicking up as they drove on through. Everyone was coming back. We had a great time. Dancing on the deck with dance music pumping through the Upstate Mountains. The deck was shaking. I felt like I was home.

June, 2010

*I*met this guy who would be the one I married. Big mistake! I'll tell you why. I tried to go along my path. He was French and Tunisian just like Azir. He had hopes and dreams to start a business but had the wrong type of Visa. He was very smart with computers. I thought this was the way to go, to marry him. After all the psychic said I will be getting married in the fall. He wanted to start up a business, and me being Aquarian saw all the possibilities. He was good in the beginning, but then it just turned bad. After we got married in November we called Immigration to check on the paperwork. Azir called. At. That. Time! I haven't heard from him in months! I couldn't answer, my "husband" yelling at me, telling me what to ask the representative, the representative being "uninformative" and the phone ringing with him calling!

I went outside and called him back.

"I'm here," he said.

I told him, "What do you think, you can just call me and I will come running like a little puppy? I got married to someone else. You're too late." I wanted to sound like I didn't care because how could I leave anyway with this guy here? Someone I didn't even like at the point I was in. And besides, I was mad at him for leaving me and not coming to see me. Plus I was mad at the way my husband was talking to me.

He says, "Okay, take care!"

Why did I do that? I thought when I hung up the phone. I could have met him in the morning. You always think of things, the way the "should" go afterward. I had to do it though. They say everything happens for a reason. I went back to life.

January 2011

Nٰews alert! Uproar in Tunisia. Unfair authority made a man set himself on fire. He didn't kill anyone else with him. This must have been such a great guy for this to cause what it did. It brought the people together to say they finally had enough. They stood up for themselves. His name should live on. But then I go back to only God taking your life. My thoughts were quickly on Azir again. Was he there? Did he hear about it? Of course, he did! He must have heard about it. Did he know this person since he is from there? My mind spinning on him again. I come home to my husband on the computer.

"Did you hear what happened in Tunisia? They are starting a revolution against the government. That's great, right?"

"Yes, of course," I said, and thought of Azir.

I would come home and there would be dishes in the sink. He would sleep on the couch all day, and when I came home I had to be quiet because he was sleeping. I couldn't disturb him because he was sleeping and he can't get any rest. He didn't work, offered nothing and did nothing. He would get mad at me because I woke him up. Really? One day I asked him to do the dishes, he yelled, "I'm a man, I don't do that!" I just looked at him and walked away. It was not for me. And to me was definitely not a man. We fought a lot. In fact, the day the world was supposed to end, May 21, 2011… again. I remember that day. My son was by his father's. This "man" is sitting there doing nothing again. I got ready to go out with my friends. As I left I told him, "Well, the world is going to end soon, so it was nice knowing you." I went to the bank and took out money, then started to go to my car. The biggest rainbow was covering over Whitestone. God truly was here with us and showed me again how beautiful our world is. It wasn't ending at all. I called Azir, he didn't answer.

I called him again while "my husband" wasn't home. Azir was at the airport. It was 4 A.M. there. I could hear the background.

"I'm sorry about the last time we spoke." I told him

"Are you still married?" he asked.

"No, it's not like that. It's kinda like business because I don't love him, I didn't even kiss him!."

"Business?" he asks. "Is he paying for you or are you paying for him?" Like he knew I was taking care of all the bills. How did he know that?! I asked him if he was coming. Now he was the one sounding like he didn't care.

I asked him, "Do you still think about me?"

"Only sometimes, not every day. I don't know if I'm coming there," he says. We said goodbye. Azir was actually cold towards me. He never spoke to me like that.

I couldn't do it anymore, take care of him, "a man," "my husband," have him ignore me in my own home, not happy on coming home to a mess. In fact, one day he was texting so much I asked to see his phone, that I paid for! He wouldn't show it to me, so I went to take it and he smashed it on the floor and kept stepping on it over and over. Hmmm, was he hiding something? Now I didn't have proof of anything. Or who this guy even is. It wasn't like 'til death do you part, it wasn't true love. I didn't want to waste my life not being true to what I wanted and how I felt I should be treated. I told him to leave. Can you believe he even said I didn't try to stop him when he left? He didn't care about me nor was he my friend. He had to go.

I spoke to Azir one other time after that. It was the fall of 2011. He was in his country shopping and told me to hold on. It sounded like he walked out of a place. Same start to the conversation, how I was, my son, how he was. Then I heard in the background, it was "Call to Prayer." Was that a sign? Should I pray for myself because of my addiction to this guy? Is this a sign that God was telling us we should be together? Or the last time I would hear his voice?

"I don't know what else to say to you," I told him. "You already know I want to see you and that's all I can say."

Those were the last words we spoke. That was the last time I heard his voice, and I never heard back from him again. In fact, his phone didn't work anymore.

My brother came to stay with me during the fall and he had a little girl that was 2 years old. I still wasn't over Azir and I looked at one of his websites. I saw he got engaged and there was a really pretty girl in the picture with him. Someone from his country. I live on the second floor. I felt my heart hit the hard, cold basement cement. My brother came home just then and asked me what was wrong. I started crying so hard. "He's marrying someone else!" My brother knew who I was talking about. He saw my tears. My poor brother with crying girls!

He ran to me and hugged me. "Oh, Kel", thank God he was there.

"He told me to wait for him, and I didn't!" Crying hysterical into him. "I went out with other guys and he knew. He knows everything! How does he know? And now he's with someone else! He doesn't want me. I'm a whore, I'm a fucking whore!" The tears came down more!

"No, Kel. You're such a good person." He held me so tight. I eventually calmed down, and my brother made sure I was okay. I remembered seeing him in my dreams before he was born. He's definitely one of my soulmates, just like my friends. He was there when I needed him.

My brother has since moved out and is taking care of his daughter now. The mother moved to another state and very rarely sees her daughter. How could a mother leave her children if you don't have to? I've dated here and there, but there is still no one who makes me feel the way I did about him. That connection. Not that I'm looking to compare him, but there was really no one who compared to the way I feel when I was next to him. And I don't want to pretend or try to make it work.

2015

I started dating someone and I had to break up with him too. We argued a lot. Over nothing. I didn't love him and I didn't want to be with him. But he always came back saying he would be different. I remember the time we were in Manhattan, I asked him to slow down since he was driving too fast. Way faster than I ever would. That caused another argument. He was trying to hurt me with his words saying how I always complain and that's why no one loves me. I know I am loved. I just didn't want to be killed with the way he drove. He was driving and yelling he didn't notice the red light and the truck stopping in front of us. He had to stop short. Trying not to argue back I see a commercial truck in front of me, mostly because we almost rear-ended it. "Azir's Trucking," it said across the back like a rainbow, even though it was in black and white. It was stopped right in front of us at a traffic light. While this guy is screaming and yelling, I toned him out. I actually smiled. Out of all the commercial trucks in all of Manhattan, there is this truck in front of me with Azir's name while the guy next to me, driving my car, is bringing me down. Like a sign from God saying to wait for that feeling Azir gave me, to wait.

In May of 2011 a major Al Qaeda was killed after he was tracked down. It was to make our world a little safer. They said they got a tip from a phone call in the beginning of the summer in 2010, the time I asked Azir if he was a terrorist. There will always be extremists looking to say what is wrong while doing something wrong themselves. Coming back for revenge. Can't the fighting and plotting to kill just stop? The ones teaming up to kill others, to hurt people. Why? That's not God's will, in any religion that believes in God.

53

I still wonder if Azir was apart of it? I think of the coincidences, him disappearing during certain times, the 2 times I saw him, him carrying a package for someone, the way he knew things about me. Why did I dream about him? I still wonder what he's doing. I still wish him happiness and thank him for making me feel what real love should feel like. That's how I feel about him. Even if he doesn't feel the same way about me …anymore. Did he get married, is he alive, was he a terrorist and now is changed, or I'm so far from that and he really had nothing to do with anything except break my heart? A lesson for me to learn, But why? I can't think about it anymore. There will always be airplanes, and how am I not to feel when I look at them and not think of him? Is he on it? Is he coming here again? Will he get killed one day when someone wants to blow themselves up while he's on one? If he really is a flight attendant?

The last dream I had of him was in January 2015. It was like we were in the woods of Pennsylvania. There were trees all around us. My head was on his shoulder while we were hugging. I felt so happy to be with him and I felt him hold me so tight I knew he loved me and we were so much in love. That's how I want to remember him. Us caring about each other even though we are so far away. Maybe he survived the beheading in our past life and we lived the rest of our lives, happy. Like it's a dream, past life, or a movie where there is a happy ending. That I feel is the only way to move on from him, thinking he was a dream. Like I said when I first met him, even if I never see him again I would have this fantasy. Knowing we had a past lifetime together filled with love is now enough for me.

I did go back to the psychic recently. When she ran the cards she mentioned Azir. The 3 of swords came up which is heartbreak. She said he did still care about me and I will see him again, but only for a short time. He does have an arranged marriage. If he were to stay with me his family would disown him and he would lose his identity. I didn't want him to be unhappy without his family but is he marrying someone he doesn't love? Like I did? She said I would get married again but couldn't see to who. Only God knows that.

If I don't find my love, the one I'm supposed to go up to heaven with, in this lifetime it's okay. I find it interesting how anything can change in a day. Sometimes it's good, sometimes it's bad. I hope there is more good. Maybe I don't need my "Adam" to go up to Heaven. Maybe it's just about us and God, Me and God that we/I have to prove our goodness to, to go "home".

I have so many people around me I love and love me in return from all over the world. Right here, where I'm supposed to be. Seeing how you are loved shows how beautiful you are. So I guess part of my wish came true. God did make me beautiful. Not about how I look but on the inside. I think being beautiful is how much you are loved and how people love you back in return. So, I no longer feel lost. I look forward to see what is in store for us.

Nostradamus held opened the book of life with blank pages. Maybe he couldn't see anymore because it wasn't bad. Our world would have no more fighting, no more hate, and no more destruction. There would be peace on earth. The rest of my wish would come true.